REMAINS TO BE SEEN
EXPLORING ANCIENT ROME

REMAINS TO BE SEEN

EXPLORING ANCIENT ROME

JOHN MALAM

EVANS BROTHERS LIMITED

First published in paperback in 2006
Evans Brothers Limited
2A Portman Mansions
Chiltern Street
London W1U 6NR

Printed in Spain by GRAFO, S.A. - Bilbao

ISBN 0 237 53154 2
13-digit ISBN (from 1 Jan 2007) 978 0 237 53154 6

Acknowledgements

The author and publishers would like to thank the following people for their valuable help and advice:

Dr Simon Esmonde-Cleary PhD, Department of Ancient History and Archaelogy, The University of Birmingham.

Andrew Selkirk and "Current Archaeology"

Margaret Sharman, author and archaelogist

Verulamium Museaum, St Albans, Herts

Illustrations: Jeffery Burn, pages 13 and 31
                     Virginia Gray pages 18, 19, 36-37
Maps: Jillie Luff, Bitmap Graphics

Editor: Jean Coppendale
Design: Neil Sayer
Production: Jenny Mulvanny

For permission to reproduce copyright material the author and publishers gratefully acknowledge the following:

Cover photograph: The Colosseum, Rome. Trip

Title page: Mosaic showing a sea god or Cernannos, god of the forest. He is seen with lobster claws or antlers coming from his head. Verulamium Museum, St Albans
page 6 Norman Tomalin, Bruce Coleman Limited **page 8** Michael Holford **page 9** (left) Laurence Hughs, The Image Bank, (right) Michael Holford **page 10** (top) e.t. archive, (bottom) michael Holford **page 11** (middle) Michael Holford, (bottom) e.t. archive, (right) Michael Holford **page 12** (top) e.t. archive, (bottom) Werner Forman Archive, Capitoline Museum, Rome **page 14** Michael Holford **page 15** (top) e.t. archive, (bottom) CM Dixon **page 16** Bridgeman Art Library **page 17** (top) CM Dixon,
(middle) Michael Holford, (bottom right) Peter Clayton **page 19** John G. Ross, Robert Harding Picture Library **page 20** e.t. archive **page 21** Adam Wolfitt, Robert Harding Picture Library **page 22** (top) English Heritage Photographic Library, (middle left) e.t. archive, (middle right) Michael Holford, (bottom) CM Dixon **page 23** (middle right) Society of Antiquaries, (bottom left) Robert Harding Picture Library, (bottomright) Museum of Antiquities **page 24** Scala **page 25** (middle left) Robert Harding Picture Library, (middle right) e.t. archive (bottom) Scala **page 26** (top) e.t. archive, (bottom) P. Nicholas, Trip **page 27** (top) Melinda Berge, Bruce Coleman Limited, (middle and bottom) Werner Forman Archive **page 28** (top) Werner Forman Archive, (middle) Michael Holford, (bottom) Verulamium Museum, St Albans **page 29** (left) e.t. archive, (right) Michael Holford **page 30** (top) Brian Philp, (bottom) J.E. Stevenson, Robert Harding Picture Library **page 31** (left) H. Rooney, Trip, (right) Tim Fisher, Life File **page 32** (top) Museo Archeologyico Nazionale, Werner Forman Archive, (bottom) Museum of London **page 33** (top) Peter Clayton, (bottom) Shrewsbury Museums **page 34** (top) e.t. archive, (middle) The British Museum, (bottom) Museum of Lodon **page 35** (middle) e.t. archive, (bottom left) Sonia Halliday Photographs, (bottom right) The British Museum **page 36** Michael Holford **page 37** Peter Clayton **page 38** (top) Michael Holford, (middle) Sonia Halliday Photographs, (bottom) Robert Harding Picture Library **page 39** (top) e.t. archive, (middle) The British Museum, (bottom) Michael Holford **page 40** (top) The Bridgeman Art Library, (bottom) Michael Holford **page 41** (top) Peter Clayton, (middle left) e.t. archive, (bottom left Sonia Halliday Photographs, (right) Topham Picture Source **page 42** (top) Robert Harding Picture Library, (bottom left) Peter Clayton, (bottom right) Adam Woolfitt, Robert Harding Picture Library **page 43** Peter Clayton **page 44** (top) Verulamium Museum, St Albans, (middle left) York Archaeological Trust, (bottom) e.t. archive **page 45** (top) Verulamium Museum, St Albans, (bottom) University of Cambridge Committe for Aerial Photography

Contents

EXPLORING ANCIENT ROME

TIMELINE OF ANCIENT ROME

and the rest of the world

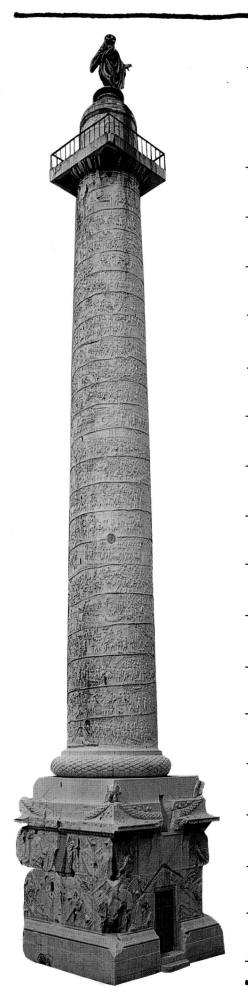

563 BC	Birth of Buddha	
551 BC	Birth of Confucius	
500 BC	Persian empire at its height	
400 BC	Athens became the leading town in Greece	
330s BC	Alexander the Great rises to power	
214 BC	Great Wall of China finished	
AD 0/0 BC	Birth of Jesus Christ	
AD 30	Jesus Christ crucified	
AD 300	Mayan Empire begins in Central America	
AD 449	Angles, Saxons and Jutes begin conquest of Britain	
AD 793	Viking raids begin in Europe	
AD 900s	Inca Empire expands in Peru	

800 BC
700 BC
600 BC
500 BC
400 BC
300 BC
200 BC
100 BC
0 BC
AD 0
AD 100
AD 200
AD 300
AD 400
AD 500
AD 600
AD 700
AD 800
AD 900
AD 1000

	753 BC	Traditional date for the founding of Rome by Romulus and Remus. Greeks colonize parts of southern Italy and Sicily.
	FROM 700 BC	Many different groups of people lived in Italy at this time, such as Etruscans and Latins.
	FROM 600 BC	The emergence of the town of Rome, from villages built on seven nearby hills.

THE ROMAN REPUBLIC 509 BC to 27 BC	509 BC	The last Etruscan king of Rome was overthrown. Roman Republic formed.
	387 BC	Rome invaded by Gauls from the north.
	264 BC	Rome became the leading town in Italy.
	264 to 146 BC	Wars between Rome and Carthage, a city in north Africa.
	73 to 71 BC	A slaves' revolt threatened Rome but was defeated.
	44 BC	Julius Caesar assassinated.

THE ROMAN EMPIRE 27 BC to AD 476	27 BC	Augustus becomes the first Roman emperor. Roman Empire formed.
	AD 64	Fire destroys a large part of Rome.
	AD 79	Mount Vesuvius destroys Pompeii and Herculaneum.
	AD 117	Roman Empire reaches its greatest extent under Emperor Trajan.
	AD 122	Rome builds frontiers at edges of the empire (such as Hadrian's Wall in Britain).
	AD 284	Emperor Diocletian divides the Roman Empire into a western half
	AD 300 to 500	and an eastern half.
	AD 313	Barbarian invaders enter the Roman Empire.
	AD 324	Emperor Constantine accepts Christianity.
	AD 330	Emperor Constantine reunites the two parts of the empire.
	AD 395	City of Constantinople (Istanbul) founded.
	AD 410	Roman Empire divided back into two parts.
	AD 476	Rome captured by the Visigoths. The last Roman emperor is overthrown. End of the Roman Empire in the west.

Dates

Roman history is usually divided into two periods called the 'Republic' and the 'Empire'. The usual way of writing dates is to refer to events before and after the birth of Jesus Christ. Anything before is said to be 'BC' (Before Christ), and anything after is 'AD' (Anno Domini, which is Latin meaning 'in the year of Our Lord').

WHO WERE THE ROMANS?

Introduction to Ancient Rome

The civilization of the Romans lasted for more than 1,000 years. From their homeland in northern Italy, the Romans created an empire that covered a large part of western and northern Europe, North Africa, and the Middle East. The people who lived within this vast area came under Roman rule – the Romans were their masters.

For hundreds of years, people from Britain in the north to Egypt in the south lived the Roman way of life. Latin, the language of the Romans, became the world's first international language. Coins stamped with portraits of Roman emperors could be spent across the empire. Roads criss-crossed the land, and along them moved armies, merchants, slaves, and travellers.

Although the Romans lived more than 1,500 years ago, we owe many things to them. Some languages spoken in Europe today, such as English, contain words that have come to us from Latin. Some of today's towns and cities can trace their origins back to ones first built by the Romans, and even concrete, a building material we think of as being 'modern', dates back to the Romans.

A Greek temple built about 450 BC at Paestum, on the west coast of Italy. The Greek name for the city was Poseidonia and the Romans later called it Paestum. The Greeks who settled at Paestum came from Sybaris, about 110 kilometres to the south east. Sybaris was another Greek city in Italy. The finest remains of Greek architecture anywhere in Italy are at Paestum. The Lucanians, a group of people who lived in the south of Italy, eventually took control of Paestum from the Greeks and in AD 273 the city became a Roman colony.

Italy

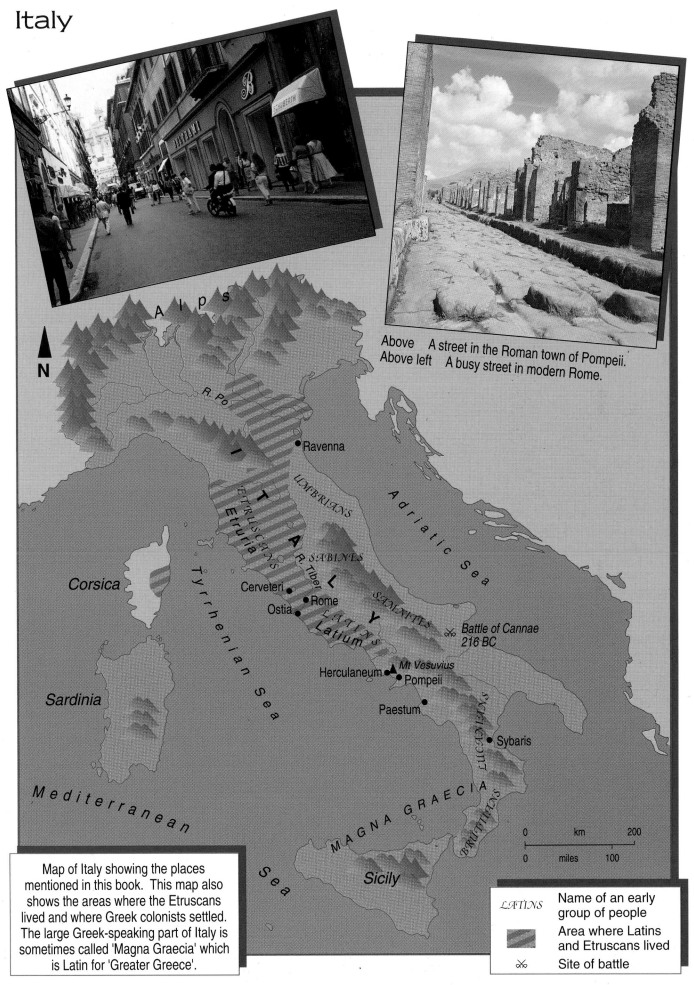

Above   A street in the Roman town of Pompeii.
Above left   A busy street in modern Rome.

Map of Italy showing the places mentioned in this book. This map also shows the areas where the Etruscans lived and where Greek colonists settled. The large Greek-speaking part of Italy is sometimes called 'Magna Graecia' which is Latin for 'Greater Greece'.

LATINS   Name of an early group of people

Area where Latins and Etruscans lived

✂   Site of battle

9

The Etruscan civilization

Central Italy was the homeland of the Etruscans. The Etruscan civilization lasted for about 600 years, from about 700 BC to 100 BC. The Ancient Greeks called them Tyrrhenians, a name which we use today for the sea to the west of their land. The Romans knew them as Tusci or Etrusci. Our modern name for the region in which they lived is Tuscany. Can you see where we get this name from? We believe the Etruscans' own name for themselves was Rasna.

The Etruscans became wealthy by trading not only with other people in Italy, but especially with the Ancient Greeks. The Etruscans had settled in a land that was rich in metal ores and

Inside a painted Etruscan tomb. The tomb was made to look like the inside of a house. This helps us to understand how Etruscan houses may have looked. The painting shows people at a banquet.

▼ This is an elaborate coffin for an Etruscan woman called Seianti who died about 150 BC (her name is written in Etruscan in the bottom right-hand corner of the coffin). She is shown reclining on a couch. When experts examined her skeleton they found that she suffered from arthritis of the jaw and had lost at least 20 teeth. They think she also had dental disease and bad breath!

timber, both of which they exported in return for finished goods, such as fine pottery from Greece.

Much of what we know about the Etruscan civilization has come from excavating their rich cemeteries, such as the one at Cerveteri, an Etruscan town about 70 kilometres northwest of Rome. The ancient burial ground contains many round mounds, which are the tombs of Cerveteri's noble and wealthy Etruscan families. The dead had been buried with valuable gifts for the next life, and since the 1830s this cemetery has been giving up its hidden secrets – to both archaeologists and illegal treasure hunters. Unfortunately, like many ancient cemeteries, tomb raiders have broken into the graves in search of treasure.

Fact File

Etruscan language and writing

The Etruscan language is a great puzzle because it is not like any other language from ancient Europe. This makes it difficult to understand, even though we can recognize all the signs in its alphabet. About 13,000 short inscriptions written in Etruscan have been found. The Etruscan alphabet was taken from one developed by the Phoenicians. Like them, the Etruscans also wrote from right to left. Because the Romans learned their alphabet from the Etruscans, it is perhaps the greatest gift they received from them.

An Etruscan model of an archer on horseback, made of bronze. When new, the metal would have been yellow in colour but after a long time buried in the ground bronze turns green.

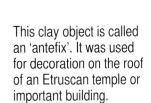

This clay object is called an 'antefix'. It was used for decoration on the roof of an Etruscan temple or important building.

The Etruscans were skilled in working with gold to make jewellery and objects such as this cup.

The rise of Rome

A pottery vessel made in the shape of an early house.

Rome began in a very small way, starting as a cluster of simple farming villages built on the tops of seven hills in the region known as Latium. The people who lived in Latium were known as Latins. By 600 BC (2,600 years ago) the villages had joined together to become the main city of Latium, with its own temples and public buildings. It is from this point onwards that we can trace the real development of the city of Rome.

For a time Rome was ruled by the powerful Etruscans from the north (see page 10) but the city's population was made up of Latin-speaking people from Latium. As Rome developed, these people grew stronger and they drove out the Etruscans. The traditional date for the overthrow of Tarquin the Proud, the last Etruscan king in Rome, is 509 BC. From then on Rome became an independent state which the Romans called 'respublica', from which we get our word 'republic'. In a republic a group of officials is elected to run a country – not just one person.

Fact File

Romulus and Remus

A legend tells of the founding of Rome. Twin baby boys called Romulus and Remus were thrown into the River Tiber by Amulius, their wicked great-uncle. Their cradle was washed up at a place near seven hills. A she-wolf found the babies and cared for them until a shepherd took them and brought them up as his own children. When they grew up, they learned how they had been abandoned by Amulius and with the help of local people they overthrew his city. They decided to build their own city on one of the seven hills, but couldn't agree which hill to choose. They argued and Romulus killed Remus. So, Romulus was left to build his city where he wished and it was named Rome after him. The traditional date given for the founding of Rome is 21 April, 753 BC.

This bronze statue of a wolf represents the she-wolf that, according to legend, suckled Romulus and Remus. It was made by an Etruscan artist about 500 BC (2,500 years ago). Although the twins are modern figures (added about AD 1500) it is likely there would have been similar figures in Roman times, but the original ones have not survived.

Early Rome was little more than a group of farming villages built on seven flat-topped hills. Each hill had its own name (see page 15). This reconstruction shows how the first village houses in the region may have looked, about 750 BC (2,750 years ago).

THE WORLD OF THE ROMANS

The Romans unite Italy

A coin with a portrait of the Carthaginian general, Hannibal. In the war against Rome he was away from his home city of Carthage for almost 35 years, most of the time fighting in Italy.

It's so hard to imagine what it must have been like during those early years for the new republic of Rome. Luckily we have the work of ancient writers whose words have survived to tell us about the struggles of the young republic.

We know from these writers that Rome was surrounded by enemies. The worst moment in Rome's early period came in 387 BC, when tribes of Gauls from northern Europe invaded Italy and attacked Rome. The Gauls entered Rome at night, but unfortunately for them they disturbed some geese who made such a noise that they woke the sleeping Romans. To make them leave the city the Romans paid the Gauls a great sum of gold. The civilized Romans regarded the Gauls as uncivilized barbarians. This invasion was a terrible setback for the Romans and it was several years before they rebuilt Rome. But when they did they put a strong wall around the city's seven hills: they weren't going to be caught out again!

From this point onwards the Romans planned to be the strongest people in the whole of Italy. For nearly 75 years they fought their enemies in the surrounding areas. Gradually local tribes came under Roman control and even the mighty Greek colonies in the south of the country could not resist the growing

Hannibal's march to Italy

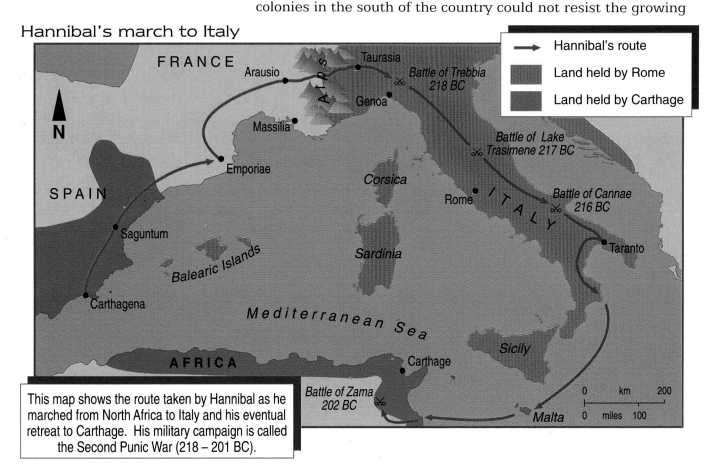

This map shows the route taken by Hannibal as he marched from North Africa to Italy and his eventual retreat to Carthage. His military campaign is called the Second Punic War (218 – 201 BC).

The seven hills of Rome

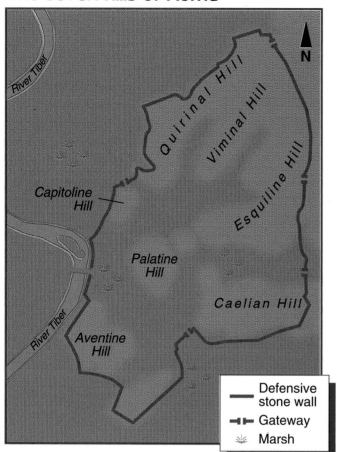

——	Defensive stone wall
⊣⊢	Gateway
⁂	Marsh

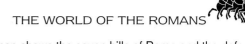

◄ This map shows the seven hills of Rome and the defensive stone wall built around them following the destruction of the city by the barbarian Gauls in 387 BC. The wall, built about 380 BC, allowed entry to the city through five gateways.

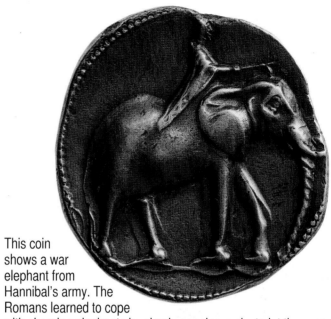

This coin shows a war elephant from Hannibal's army. The Romans learned to cope with charging elephants by simply opening ranks to let them pass through. Elephants did not play a great part in the war between the two sides.

strength of the Romans. By 264 BC their plan had worked. The Romans had become the strongest force in Italy, and Rome was the most important town.

A dagger (with its scabbard) used by the Gauls against the Romans.

Fact File

Hannibal – enemy of Rome

In 241 BC Rome gained control of Sicily from Carthage, a powerful city in North Africa. Hannibal, a Carthaginian general, decided to punish Rome. In 218 BC he led an army from North Africa to Spain, across the Pyrenees, and over the snow-covered Alps. About 20,000 foot soldiers, 6,000 cavalry and 12 war elephants survived the long march to fight the Romans in Italy. At the battle of Cannae in 216 BC about 50,000 Romans were killed – the worst defeat in Rome's entire history. The Romans found a leader to match Hannibal, a general called Scipio. He forced Hannibal back to Africa where he defeated him at the battle of Zama in 202 BC. Then, about 50 years later the Romans destroyed Carthage itself. Its buildings were pulled down and the ground sown with salt so that nothing would grow there again. The wars between Carthage and Rome are called the Punic Wars (Punic is from a Latin word meaning 'Phoenician', for the people who lived in Carthage).

Julius Caesar, the conquering general

Julius Caesar was born in 100 BC in Rome. He came from a leading Roman family and when he was only 20 years old he won the army's top honour for saving the life of a comrade during a battle in Asia. He returned to Rome where he made a name for himself as a great speaker. He became popular with both the senators and the ordinary citizens of Rome. Once, on a trip to the Greek island of Rhodes, he was captured by pirates and only released after a ransom was paid. He later returned to Rhodes, caught the pirates and had them executed.

In 60 BC Caesar was elected consul – the most important job in the Roman Republic (see page 19). It was from this point that Caesar's military career really began. In 58 BC he took charge of the Roman army in Gaul (a large area covering present-day France and Belgium). The tribes in this area were defeated. Then in 55 and 54 BC he invaded southern Britain – but his stay there was short. He had to return to Gaul to stop a rebellion amongst the tribes. Then news reached Caesar that Pompey, another Roman general, was plotting against him in Rome.

In 49 BC Caesar returned to Rome and was made welcome by the people. Pompey fled to Egypt where he was murdered. Caesar was popular with the people and he was declared 'Dictator of Rome'. This made him very powerful – but it also made him many enemies. Some senators feared he was becoming too powerful and their fear led them to assassinate him on 15 March, 44 BC.

For several years after Julius Caesar's death there was disorder in Rome. Peace was eventually restored to the city by Caesar's nephew, Augustus, who became the first Roman emperor (see page 18).

A statue of Julius Caesar dressed in the uniform of a military leader. Under his leadership Roman territory expanded. Caesar was popular with the army and the people, but not with the senators – they plotted his murder.

A marble statue known as the 'Dying Gaul', made by the Romans in honour of a victory over the Gauls of northern Europe.

A portrait of Julius Caesar on a coin. His coins were the first ones to show a portrait of a living Roman. The inscription reads 'CAESAR: DICT PERPETUO' which means 'Caesar, Dictator for Life'. He is shown wearing a wreath of laurel leaves which was a symbol of victory and peace.

Republic and empire

The Roman Republic (509 to 27 BC)

At first Rome was a monarchy ruled by a king. But in 509 BC Rome changed from a monarchy to a republic. The Roman Republic lasted for almost 500 years. Being a republic meant that no individual had too much power, unlike when the Romans were ruled by a king. The most important people in the Roman Republic were two men called 'consuls'. They kept their jobs for one year at a time. By having regular elections different people could become one of the consuls each year. The consuls were advised by experienced politicians called 'senators'. There were about 600 senators – mostly rich men from powerful Roman families. The group of senators was called the Senate and it made important decisions on political, military and legal matters. The Senate became Rome's government. This system worked well in the time of the Roman Republic but it lost much of its power during the Roman Empire when emperors took more and more control.

Roman citizens were divided into 'patricians' (rich men such as nobles) and 'plebeians' (poor men such as farmers and shopkeepers).

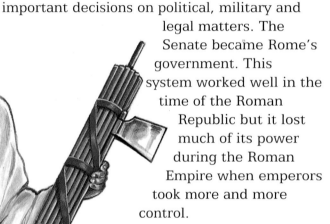

This bundle of rods containing an axe, tightly bound with a red strap, was called a 'fasces'. It was an ancient sign of authority, first used by the Etruscans. Later, Rome's early kings adopted it and during the Roman Republic the consuls took turns to hold the 'fasces'.

18

The Roman Empire (27 BC to AD 476)

During the time of the Roman Republic, Roman armies conquered lands throughout Europe, Africa and the Middle East. Between 100 BC and 50 BC civil wars broke out with Romans fighting Romans. With strong generals at the head of the army the Roman senators thought that one of them wanted to become king. They feared Julius Caesar the most and had him murdered (see page 16). But this terrible act only caused more fighting. It was Caesar's nephew, Octavian, who finally restored law and order to Rome, and in 27 BC he became the first Roman emperor – a king by another name. He is better known as Augustus, the title he was given. In the 500 years of the Roman Empire, Rome had nearly 100 emperors.

This is how a Roman army standard may have looked. A standard was an important symbol. To lose one was a disgrace. The letters SPQR were a Latin abbreviation for 'Senatus Populus Que Romanus', which meant 'The Senate and the People of Rome'. The decorations on a standard were awarded for battle victories and bravery.

Gaius Julius Caesar Octavianus, better known as Rome's first emperor, Augustus. The rod in his left hand is an army standard which the Romans had lost in battle. Augustus succeeded in recovering it and that event is shown on his finely carved breastplate. Statues of Augustus were set up all over the Roman Empire.

The Roman Empire

In AD 113 a war memorial was erected in Rome to commemorate Emperor Trajan's victory over the Dacians (in modern day Romania). Known as 'Trajan's Column' it is 30 metres high (see page 6) and is decorated with carvings that run in a spiral. The carvings tell how Trajan conquered the Dacians, as in this detail where people take cover inside a fort. If the spiral was unwound, the carvings would form a picture about 200 metres long!

It was after the Romans had become the most powerful people in Italy that they began to add foreign lands to their territory. From then on their empire began to grow. In 146 BC the Carthaginians were defeated and Rome took over all their land in North Africa and the Mediterranean (see page 15). In the same year Greece came under Roman control. Not every land was conquered by force. Some countries asked Rome to help them settle disputes. In return they promised to obey Rome. Other countries became part of the Roman Empire when their rulers gave them to Rome, as happened with some lands in the Middle East. The Romans used the word 'provincia' to describe their foreign lands, from which our own word 'province' comes.

The Roman Empire was at its most extensive in the reign of Emperor Trajan who was emperor from AD 98 to AD 117. But having a great empire had its problems. It was expensive to control and look after so many provinces. Soldiers had to be stationed abroad in case a province rebelled – and the soldiers had to be paid. Expensive roads and bridges had to be built. Even

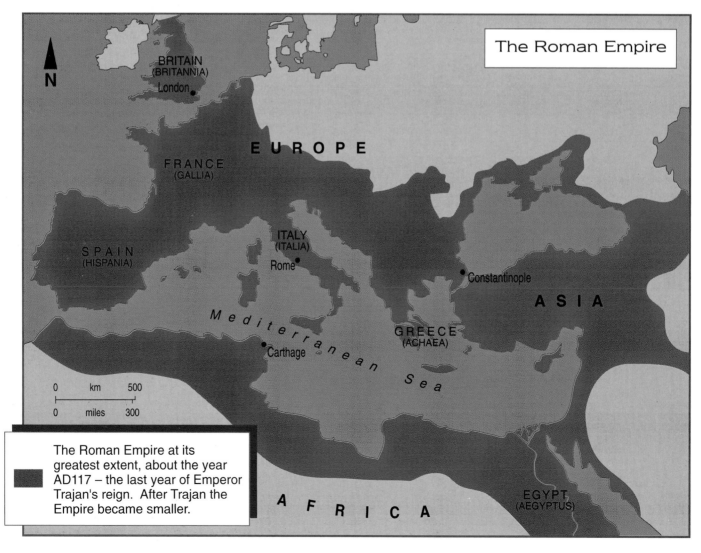

The Roman Empire at its greatest extent, about the year AD117 – the last year of Emperor Trajan's reign. After Trajan the Empire became smaller.

In AD 118 a revolt amongst the northern tribes in Britain was stopped by the Romans. In AD 122 Emperor Hadrian called for a stone and turf wall to be built to protect Roman Britain from the trouble-makers in the north. Parts of it were painted white so it could be seen from a distance. Hadrian's Wall became the northern boundary of the Roman Empire for 250 years. It ran for 120 kilometres and crossed the country from coast to coast.

though taxes were collected from the provinces it was often not enough to meet the costs of actually looking after them. Rome found itself under more and more pressure and just over 100 years after Trajan had increased the empire to its greatest extent, it began to break up.

The empire was surrounded by Rome's enemies, whom the Roman's called 'barbarians'. To the Romans, these people were uncivilized, warlike trouble-makers. But the fact was they outnumbered the Romans, and when they began to make claims on the Romans' territory, it was only a matter of time before the empire collapsed under the strain (see page 42).

Fact File

Goods from the Empire

The Roman Empire was rich in goods that Rome wanted and valuable supplies were taken to Rome from distant lands. This meant that exotic and rare produce could be enjoyed by wealthy Romans. Here are some of the goods sent to Rome, and the areas from which they came.

Goods	Land
Gold	Balkans, Spain, Wales
Grain	Egypt, Spain, North Africa
Honey	Spain
Horses	Spain
Lead	Britain
Marble	Greece, Turkey, North Africa
Olive oil	Greece, Spain, Turkey, North Africa
Papyrus	Egypt
Perfume	Asia
Pottery	France, Greece, Spain
Silk	China
Slaves	Britain, Germany, Greece, Turkey
Spices	Asia
Timber	Germany
Tin	Britain
Wine	France, Spain, Middle East

Ancient Rome at war

Housesteads Fort, where soldiers who patrolled Hadrian's Wall in northern Britain were stationed. You can see the remains of the fort's buildings – its headquarters, commander's house, barracks, granaries, hospital, toilets and gateways.

The Romans needed a large army to protect their empire from attackers – both from outside the empire and from rebellions within it. All men who were Roman citizens aged between 17 and 46 could be called on to join the army. They joined large army units called 'legions', and the soldiers themselves were called 'legionaries'. Each legion had about 5,300 foot soldiers, divided into ten smaller units called 'cohorts'. Even smaller units were called 'centuries' which had 80 men in them (at first they had 100 men

How a Roman ▶ legionary soldier dressed. His body and shoulders were protected by plates of steel armour and he wore a steel helmet which gave good protection to his head and neck. His kilt was formed from leather strips covered with metal, and on his feet were thick-soled leather sandals. When he was on the march he carried food, tools and even cooking equipment.

▲
The soldiers in this mosaic picture have shields for defence and javelins for attack.

When advancing, soldiers covered themselves with their shields. This formation was called a 'testudo' or tortoise.

each). The smallest units had eight men each – the so-called 'tent-parties'. These were groups who shared tents and sleeping quarters together.

Men from the Roman provinces, and who were therefore not classed as Roman citizens, could also join the army. They were called 'auxiliaries' and their numbers made up almost half the army. After they had completed their military service they were granted Roman citizenship, which was very precious to them.

Soldiers joined the army for 25 years and in all that time they could not marry. On leaving the army they were given some land on which they could start a small farm.

The Roman army was successful not just because it was well organized and its soldiers were well trained, but because its generals planned their battles with great care. Battles were usually planned weeks or months in advance. Scouts spied on the enemy, bringing back information about the enemy's strength and weapons. With this information in their hands, the Roman generals then worked out the best way for their attack. Sometimes towns were besieged by the Roman army which camped outside. A siege could last months, until the people in the town surrendered through lack of food and supplies.

Fact File

Heavy weapons

Just like a modern army, there were surprises in store for an unsuspecting, and unfortunate, enemy! The 'carroballista' and the 'onager' were two kinds of heavy weapon. Both were operated by strong springs. The 'carroballista' could be mounted on a cart, pulled by two ponies. Ten men were needed to fire the weapon which shot long-range arrows or iron bolts deep behind enemy lines. The 'onager' was a catapult that could hurl large boulders over a great distance. Weapons such as these were used to weaken an enemy before any hand-to-hand fighting began.

The head of an iron bolt fired from a powerful Roman weapon called a 'carroballista', a type of crossbow. It was found lodged in the spine of a man who had died defending a British community from a Roman attack.

A Roman helmet with a face mask like this was not worn in battle. It would have been worn on special occasions only, such as parades.

This model shows how an 'onager' probably looked. It could throw large rocks over long distances and was used during seiges. Its name means 'wild ass' after the kicking action when it was fired.

Rome – capital of the empire

Emperor Augustus, the first Roman emperor (see page 19) began a major rebuilding programme in Rome. He said, 'I found Rome a city of bricks but I left it a city of marble'. How right he was!

The picture below shows Rome at its grandest, about the year AD 300, when one million people lived there. With its network of roads, its groups of houses and its large, important buildings, it had all the features of a successful city – and many of the problems, too. There was poverty and many ordinary citizens lived in awful conditions. Successive Roman emperors had built larger and grander buildings but neglected to build better housing for the poor. Greedy landlords took advantage of this situation. They built extra floors on the houses they owned and squeezed even more people inside. More people meant more rent for the owners. This type of housing resembled small blocks of flats – but without any running water, no toilets and with little natural light.

How Rome may have looked in AD 300. Visitors would have been impressed by its magnificent public buildings – but they would not have seen its slums where most of the population lived.

Ancient Rome was a city of contrasts – like many cities in the world today. The rich lived well and enjoyed the benefits of being in the capital. But for most people life was hard, with a shortage of work, poor living conditions and a short life. You were very old if you reached the age of 50!

Trajan's Market was a large market-place, or 'forum', in the centre of Rome. It had law courts, shops, offices, libraries and meeting rooms.

A model of a block of flats from Ostia, the port of Rome. There were many blocks like this in Rome. The ground floor was filled with shops and the upper storeys provided poor quality, overcrowded housing. For safety reasons they could not be built higher than about 20 metres.

Fact File

Rome on fire

In AD 64 a fire burned for nine days and destroyed a large part of Rome. The emperor at this time was Nero and he may have ordered his servants to start it. Why? Nero wanted a grand palace and after the fire he bought the burnt-out parts of the city. He cleared the land and built a palace which he called the 'Golden House'. It was adorned with gold plate, mother-of-pearl and statues taken from Greek cities. 'I have begun,' he said, 'to be housed as a man ought to be.' When Nero learned that people were saying he had started the fire on purpose, he blamed it on Christians, who were then a new religious sect (see page 40). Many Christians were executed on Nero's orders. He became very unpopular, and faced with a rebellion he committed suicide at the age of 32.

Emperor Nero almost bankrupted Rome with his expensive schemes to rebuild the city after the great fire.

Pompeii – a Roman town

The Romans kept guard dogs, as this mosaic from Pompeii shows. One mosaic even bore the message 'cave canem' which is Latin for beware of the dog!

Pompeii's streets formed a grid pattern of squares and rectangles. Houses and shops were built inside the squares. Each square was called an 'insula', meaning 'island', because it was surrounded by streets. Most Roman towns followed a grid pattern.

About 200 kilometres south of Rome is the small Roman town of Pompeii. Nearby is an active volvano, Mount Versuvius.

On 24 August, AD 79, Mount Vesuvius erupted. The volcano had been quiet for years and the people living in towns nearby could not have expected it to explode with such destructive force. The day had begun as a public holiday but within hours the towns of Pompeii, Herculaneum, Stabiae and Oplontis were destroyed.

Lava pebbles, pumice, ash and poisonous gases rained down on Pompeii, burying the town under about four metres of debris. Of the town's 20,000 inhabitants, about 2,000 were killed. Those that escaped lost all their possessions and were made homeless.

The destruction of Pompeii was a natural disaster, but it has preserved a complete Roman town for archaeologists to study. Not only are buildings preserved, but so are traces of the people who lived and worked in them, such as the contents of shops, unfinished meals on tables and wall paintings. Seeds found in gardens reveal what plants the people of Pompeii grew. Some of the buildings have graffiti scribbled on their walls. A Roman with a sense of humour wrote on one wall, 'Everyone writes on walls except me!' Even the victims of the eruption have been found, buried under the debris from Vesuvius. Although their bodies rotted

A person who died during the eruption of Mount Vesuvius. The body was covered by ash and over the centuries it has vanished, leaving a body-shaped space behind. By pumping plaster of Paris into the space the exact shape of the body can be found.

Fact File

Herculaneum

Herculaneum was a Roman seaside town near Mount Vesuvius, about 16 kilometres away from Pompeii. Some of Rome's leading families had luxurious houses there where they went for holidays. When Vesuvius erupted this wealthy town was submerged under 20 metres of hot lava which flowed out of the volcano. It cooled to set as hard as rock. Most of the inhabitants managed to escape – leaving their belongings behind. Herculaneum became a 'time capsule', sealed from the outside world. People forgot about the town until 1709 when a workman digging a well found blocks of marble buried deep under the ground. From this time onwards, Herculaneum has gradually been uncovered and the work still goes on today.

The street in the left of this picture has a stepping stone in it for pedestrians to use when crossing the road. Wheeled vehicles could pass over the stone. Look for the ruts their wheels have made beyond the stone.

away long ago their shapes have been preserved as hollow spaces which can be filled with plaster of Paris. When the plaster has set the volcanic debris is removed, revealing the ghostly shapes of people and animals just as they were the moment disaster struck.

The Romans didn't use wallpaper, but they did paint the walls of their houses. These paintings are in a house at Pompeii.

Everyday life in towns

▲
Most Roman towns had public baths. This example is at Pompeii and was used as a steam room, just like our saunas are today. Hot air circulated under the floor and along channels behind the walls. The temperature was high and a Roman writer said it was 'like being on a bonfire!'

What sort of lives did people lead in Roman towns? Most towns were built to the same basic design. At their heart was a large open area called the 'forum'. It was the town's market-place, where traders sold produce and where business people met. Around the sides of the forum were shops and offices. Just like our own markets today, the Roman forum would have been a noisy place, packed with busy people – and bargains if you were lucky! Next door to the forum was the 'basilica', a large public building for the town's officials. It was similar to our present-day town hall.

A vital necessity of town life was the water supply. Without adequate supplies of fresh, clean water, disease could spread quickly in the cramped and dirty conditions. Water was carried into towns by underground pipes and also by special bridges called 'aqueducts' (see page 30). Wells were dug inside towns. To stop them from drying out they

▲
This bronze object, called a 'strigil', was used in Roman baths. Bathers rubbed oil on to their bodies and then scraped it off, with all the dirt, using a strigil.

Pots such as these were used throughout the Roman Empire for carrying wine, oil, honey and for grinding food in. To the left is a pot full of holes for straining liquids.

often had to be deepened – a dangerous job for a workman.

At the end of the day some people would go to the town's baths – which to us would be like a mixture between a swimming pool, a sauna and an exercise gym! Inside were three types of bath: cold, warm and hot. The visitor would spend time in each before finishing with a massage. If you wanted to meet friends and catch up on the day's news and gossip, then a trip to the baths was essential!

Meal times were another occasion when friends and family came together. Romans ate their meals reclining on couches – not sitting at tables as we do. Another difference is that they didn't use cutlery – instead they used bread to scoop up their food. An important meal might consist of shellfish, eggs, snails and vegetables, followed by fish and roasted birds. Then came venison, hare, pork and more fish. Finally, many kinds of fruit were served. Wine was drunk with the meal. Guests who had eaten too much could leave the room to be sick – before returning, ready to start eating all over again. This way, a Roman banquet was guaranteed to last a long time!

Fact File

Country life

Wealthy Romans often owned a house in a town and one in the country too. The country house was called a 'villa'. But the villa was more than just a second home. It was a farm, with the villa at the centre of an estate. Slaves were used to work the land and their conditions could be hard, especially if they worked for a cruel owner. Some slaves worked for caring masters, and as a reward for good service they might be given their freedom, and so become Roman citizens. Villas and their estates were an essential part of Roman life, since the food they produced was supplied to nearby towns. Cereals, cabbages, lettuces, tomatoes, carrots, olives, apples, figs, pears and grapes were grown. Pork was the most popular meat, so herds of pigs were raised. Sheep were kept for wool and milk, and chickens for eggs and meat. Pigeons were bred for winter meat. The Romans didn't know about sugar, so they used honey instead. You would always see bee hives on a farm estate.

A wall painting of a villa in the countryside.

A mosaic picture of a group of people reclining at a meal while a musician entertains them with music.

ROMAN ACHIEVEMENTS

Roads and buildings

Milestones were placed along roads, giving information about distances between places. One Roman mile measured 1,472 metres (one mile today measures 1,609 metres). This milestone was found on the Fosse Way near Leicester, England. It was erected during the reign of Emperor Hadrian in AD 120.

Towns throughout the Roman Empire were connected by a network of roads. It was vital that the road system worked well, otherwise important news could not be passed between places. And as Rome was at the centre of communications for the empire, all roads led to it – eventually! In 20 BC Emperor Augustus erected the famous 'golden milestone' in Rome. It was a marble column on to which were fixed golden plates with distances from Rome to towns throughout the empire.

Roads were often built by the army so that soldiers could be moved quickly across new land. Some roads were frontiers marking the new boundaries of the expanding Roman Empire. Gradually, as any danger passed, minor roads were built branching off from the main roads, taking traffic further inland.

Experts believe the Romans built over 90,000 kilometres of road. About 16,000 kilometres were built in Britain alone. Some modern roads are built on top of Roman ones – so we are still using the same routes 2,000 years after the Romans first planned them!

This aqueduct carried drinking water across the River Gard and into the French city of Nîmes. Water flowed inside a channel along the very top of the aqueduct, above the small arches. The word aqueduct comes from the Latin 'aquam ducere' meaning 'to carry water'. Look for the people in the photograph to see just how big this aqueduct is.

Fact File

Concrete

If you think concrete is a modern invention, then think again! The Romans combined ash, lime mortar, sand and gravel to produce the first concrete in the world – a waterproof and incredibly hard material. Concrete revolutionized the Roman building industry. Because liquid concrete could be poured into moulds it was possible to cast it into lots of different shapes. Architects were able to design new types of building using concrete and two famous Roman buildings could not have been built without it – the Colosseum (see page 38) and the Pantheon.

Across soft ground

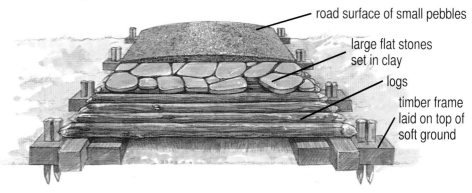

road surface of small pebbles

large flat stones set in clay

logs

timber frame laid on top of soft ground

Across hard ground

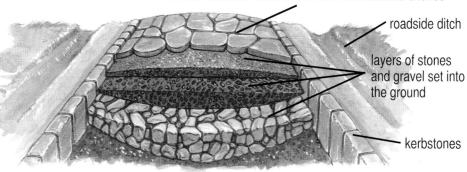

road surface of large flat stones set in a 'camber' (curve) so that rainwater could run off into the roadside ditches

roadside ditch

layers of stones and gravel set into the ground

kerbstones

Cross-sections through two types of Roman road, showing the different methods of building them.

This temple building in Rome is called the Pantheon. It was built about AD 120 and its dome was made from overlapping rings of concrete. The hole at the top of the dome let daylight into the building.

▲
Seen from above, the straightness of a Roman road can really be appreciated. This road is in Wales. Roads like this were plotted by surveyors and wherever possible they took the most direct course between two points – which is why they were so straight.

Language and writing

This wall painting from Pompeii shows a girl holding a set of wooden writing tablets like the one in the picture below. In her right hand is a writing instrument called a 'stylus'. Note how she holds it.

The language the Romans used was called Latin. In its time Latin was probably the most widely spoken language in the world. A traveller could go from Britain to the Middle East and north Africa, knowing that he could use Latin and be understood. If a traveller used Latin on the same trip today, very few people would understand them! Latin is the ancestor of many modern languages, which is why there are similar words in different languages.

How did the Romans write their language down? We know a lot about this because there is much evidence to study. There are literally thousands of inscriptions to read. Some are very impressive and are carved on important buildings, while others are more humble such as ones carved on tombstones or written on personal property. It is often the personal inscriptions that are the most interesting, such as the words 'Faustine vivas' (meaning long live Faustinus) written on a silver spoon found amongst a hoard of Roman treasure from Suffolk, England. Experts think it is a reference to the wealthy Faustinus family who lived in that area about 1,500 years ago. From these two Latin words it is possible to link the treasure to a real Roman family – a very rare and exciting event!

A collection of Roman writing implements: a wooden tablet which held a thin layer of wax, metal pens for scratching into the wax and two inkwells.

Since 1973 wooden writing tablets have been excavated at Vindolanda, a fort on Hadrian's Wall in northern Britain. Waterlogged soil has preserved the tablets, together with traces of writing which are 1,800 years old. These tablets were written on in ink, not scratched on as with the tablets coated with wax. From them we can learn about life in a fort at the very edge of the Roman Empire.

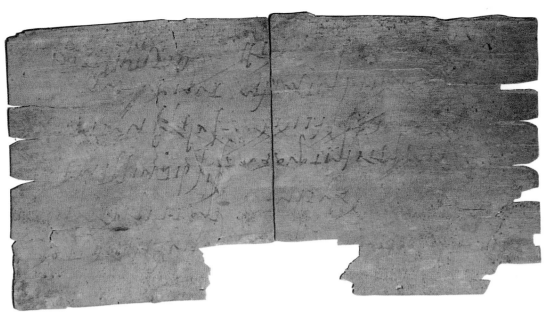

One type of material the Romans wrote on was papyrus – a kind of paper made from layers of reeds. Instead of books with separate pages, the Romans used papyrus rolls. When fully opened the rolls could be several metres long. A finer type of writing material was parchment (also called vellum). This was made from sheep and goat skins. Anything written on papyrus or parchment became a permanent record. For everyday notes and letters the Romans used small tablets of wood, coated with wax. A metal rod called a stylus was used to scratch into the wax. When the message had been read, the blunt end of the stylus smoothed the wax over, and the wax could be written on again.

Fact File

Inscriptions

Roman inscriptions can look like a line of initials, because common words were shortened to abbreviations – often single letters. Names such as Aulus, Quintus and Sextus were abbreviated to A, Q and S. Each letter had its own meaning and to the trained eye can be read quite easily.

Latin abbreviations are still used today. In Britain, for example, the country's coins are minted with the Latin abbreviation 'D.G.REG.F.D'. In full, this stands for 'Dei Gratia Regina Fidei Defensor' which means 'by the grace of God, the Queen, Defender of the Faith'.

Roman cities often had inscriptions carved in stone to record the visit of an emperor or a famous general. This inscription from the city of Viroconium (Wroxeter) in Shropshire, England, refers to the rebuilding of the city during the reign of Emperor Hadrian. Look for his name. It dates from about AD 130 and a master craftsman from Rome may have cut the letters.

Crafts of the Romans

A gold necklace from Pompeii, decorated with precious stones and mother-of-pearl.

This brooch is called a cameo. It was made from a semi-precious stone which was carved to reveal the different layers of colour. The cameo shows a portrait of Emperor Augustus.

Jewellery

Gold and silver were used for rings, anklets, bracelets, chains, earrings, tiaras and brooches. Both men and women wore rings on their fingers, often between the first and second finger joints, not between the second and third. This explains why Roman rings can be tiny, looking as if they were meant for children rather than adults. Children wore a 'bulla'. This was an ornament around the neck designed to protect them from misfortune.

Pottery

Pottery-making was carried out on a large scale, and some areas of the Roman Empire specialized in certain types of pottery. Large, round-bodied pots called amphorae were produced in Spain. These were used to hold wine, olive oil or fish sauce. Red pottery with a shiny surface was made in France. Millions of pieces of this fine tableware were made, some of which were stamped with their potters' names. In Britain, in the area around Oxford, mixing bowls were made from a white clay. Sharp pieces of grit on the inside of the bowls made their surfaces rough for grinding and crushing food. Some of these bowls also had their makers' names stamped on to them.

Pottery bowls made from a fine red clay. This type of pottery is called Samian ware and was made in France. The name of the potter is stamped in the centre of the large bowl.

Paintings and mosaics

Roman buildings were often highly decorated on the inside. At Pompeii (see page 26) wall paintings are well preserved and show us that the Romans liked to decorate their rooms with colourful pictures. Mosaics were pictures too, usually on the floor but sometimes on the walls, made from tiny cubes of coloured stone called tesserae. Pieces of pottery or glass were also used in mosaic pictures. Different coloured tesserae were used to make striking, hard-wearing designs.

A wall painting from Pompeii of a man dressed in a toga, the usual one-piece garment worn by Roman men. A helper assisted the wearer to put his toga on. The toga was usually made of uncoloured wool.

This mosaic found in Sicily shows young girls exercising in bikinis.

Fact File

What did they wear?

The Romans wore different types of clothes in different climates and for various occasions. One of the best known items of Roman clothing was the toga which may have begun with the Etruscans (see page 10), as it was similar to their wrap-around cloak. The toga was at first worn by both Roman men and women, but it seems to have gone out of fashion with women at an early date. Woven from wool, the toga was semi-circular in shape and about five metres long. It was draped over the left shoulder, around the body and then over the right arm. A toga worn by a boy between the ages of 14 and 16 usually had a purple border added to its long straight edge.

The standard garment for a married Roman woman was the 'stola'. This was a long, folded gown, with or without sleeves, which reached to the ground. Brooches fastened the stola to the underclothes. Unmarried women wore a plain tunic.

This blue glass vase, coated with carved white glass, was found in a tomb near Rome where it originally held the ashes from a cremation. Today it is known as the Portland Vase, named after the Duke of Portland who once owned it. In 1845 it was smashed to pieces by a visitor to the British Museum – but the repair work is so good you cannot see the joins.

RELIGION AND FESTIVALS

Gods and goddesses

Roman religion grew out of people's belief in spirits, which were believed to control and guide everyday life. In time the spirits became the gods and goddesses of the Romans.

Many aspects of Roman life were governed by particular gods. People were superstitious and prayed to the gods for protection and good fortune. Sacrifices of animals, usually cattle, sheep, pigs, goats and doves, were made. Priests killed the animals with special knives, and officials examined the entrails (insides) for signs of good or bad luck. For example, the colour and size of the liver was said to show if the gods were pleased or angry.

With lots of different gods, many festivals to celebrate and with no single god that everyone believed in, Roman religion must have seemed very confusing. When a new religion began in Palestine, in the first century AD, it probably seemed like a local cult that would eventually disappear, as so many others had before it. This religion was called Christianity and rather than disappearing without trace it grew and spread so that by the fourth century AD it became the official religion of the empire, and worship of the old Roman gods was banned (see page 40).

A coin showing the god Janus. He was shown with two faces – one looking back to the old and the other looking forward to the new. The month of January is named after him because it represents the passing of the old year and the start of the new year.

Diana
She was goddess of the moon and hunting.

Vulcan
He was the god of fire and metal-working.

Ceres
She was goddess of agriculture.

Jupiter
He was the king of the gods whose symbol was an eagle.

Fact File

Temples

Roman temples were copied from those of the Ancient Greeks and Etruscans. Rows of columns lined the sides of a temple and inside was a statue of the god whose temple it was. The statue was often covered in gold and jewellery. In the courtyard at the front of the temple was an altar at which sacrifices would be made.

A Roman temple in Nîmes, southern France.

Roman gods and goddesses

This table shows the most important gods and goddesses. Some were taken by the Romans from other religions. For example, the twelve most important gods worshipped by the Ancient Greeks were absorbed into the Roman religion. These Greek gods are marked with an asterisk (*). The Romans gave them new names but mostly left their duties unchanged.

1. Apollo*   god of sun, light and good fortune.
2. Bacchus   god of wine.
3. Ceres*   goddess of agriculture.
4. Diana*   goddess of the moon and hunting.
5. Janus   god of new beginnings – the first hour of the day, the first day of the month, and so on.
6. Jupiter*   god of the sky and king of the gods.
7. Juno*   goddess of marriage and women.
8. Mars*   god of war.
9. Mercury*   god of trade and communications.
10. Minerva*   goddess of art and war.
11. Neptune*   god of the sea.
12. Pluto   god of the underworld.
13. Saturn   god of agriculture.
14. Venus*   goddess of love and beauty.
15. Vesta*   goddess of the family and the hearth.
16. Vulcan*   god of fire and metal-working.

Juno
She was the queen of the gods whose symbols were a peacock and a pomegranate.

Neptune
He was the god of the sea.

Mercury
He was the god of trade and communications.

Games and gladiators

A lightly-armoured gladiator known as a 'retiarius'. He is holding a trident and a short sword.

The Colosseum in Rome is the most famous Roman amphitheatre (see front cover). Its name comes from a huge statue (called a colossus) of the Emperor Nero that once stood nearby. 50,000 spectators filled the Colosseum to watch gladiator fights and animal hunts. The floor of the arena is now missing and you can see the underground passages where gladiators and animals waited before a contest.

Chariot races

In Rome was the 'Circus Maximus' (this means the Great Circus). This open-air building was an oval racetrack for horse-drawn chariots. It was 600 metres long and had seats for 250,000 spectators. Races were usually seven laps of the track – about eight kilometres. Chariot drivers could earn a lot of money – for themselves and their managers. One charioteer, Diocles, was in 4,257 races in 24 years. He won 1,462 of them!

Gladiator fights

Tough slaves and criminals fought in front of audiences in open-air arenas called amphitheatres. The fighters were called gladiators (this means swordsmen). They were trained to fight in different ways and with different types of equipment. A 'secutor' gladiator had heavy armour and a sword. A lightly-armoured 'retiarius' gladiator had a net, a trident and a short sword. A 'secutor' usually fought a 'retiarius' – the Romans thought the differences between them made the fight good to watch. Gladiators often fought to the death.

Animal hunts

A fighter who killed wild animals in front of an audience was called a 'bestiarius'. Animals such as elephants, lions, panthers, leopards and boars were caught and taken to Rome. In the city's amphitheatres beast-hunters stalked them as if they were in the wild before killing them.

A mosaic picture of a lion hunt. Exotic animals were caught in the wild and taken to Rome where they were killed in mock hunts in amphitheatres. Wild animals were especially collected in north Africa.

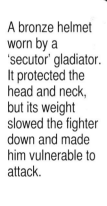

A bronze helmet worn by a 'secutor' gladiator. It protected the head and neck, but its weight slowed the fighter down and made him vulnerable to attack.

Roman chariots were small and delicately made. They were usually pulled by teams of two or four horses. This is a model made from bronze and may have been a child's toy.

Fact File

Thumbs up or down?

Sometimes a gladiator could appeal to the audience for his life to be spared. This usually only happened if the fight had been a good one and the defeated man had fought well. He appealed to the crowd by raising a finger to them. At this sign the crowd would respond by either giving a 'thumbs pressed' sign (pressing a thumb into the palm of the other hand) or by a 'thumbs turned' sign (pointing a thumb down to the ground). The 'thumbs pressed' sign meant mercy was given, but the 'thumbs turned' sign meant no mercy and the poor man was killed. The thumb may have represented the sword – so touching your palm was indicating the sword should be put back in its sheath, whereas turning it down was like swishing a sword through the air. Our own thumbs up and thumbs down signs (for 'good' and 'bad') may be connected with this Roman tradition.

Christianity

A mosaic picture of Jesus Christ, found in a Roman building in Dorset, England. He is shown dressed in a Roman toga and behind his head is an important symbol used by early Christians. It is an X and P which are the first two letters of Christ's name in Greek. These letters are called 'chi' and 'rho' and so this symbol is called the 'chi-rho' sign.

The Romans usually tolerated 'foreign' religions, so much so that they took over other peoples' gods and worshipped them as their own (see page 36). But there was one religion they found hard to accept – Christianity. This new religion was worshipped by followers of Jesus Christ who had lived and died in the early years of the first century AD in the Roman province of Judaea, an area that covers modern Israel, Palestine and Lebanon.

Why did the Romans fear Christianity? Christians believed in only one god. They did not worship Roman gods and more importantly they did not believe the emperor was a living god. These were seen as signs of rebellion against Rome, and Christians were rounded up and killed – often in front of Roman audiences in amphitheatres where they were savaged by wild animals (see page 38). The Romans could not understand why anyone would want to follow the teachings of Jesus Christ – a man whom they had regarded as a common criminal and whom they had executed. Christianity was banned but its followers found ways of passing on their new religion to others.

Christianity proved to be a strong religion and Roman attempts to wipe it out failed. Rather than disappearing (like other cults had) it spread throughout the Roman Empire. In the fourth century AD, Emperor Constantine accepted that Christianity was going to survive and in AD 313 he made it the official religion of Rome. This meant that after 300 years of persecution, Christians could at last openly follow the teachings of Jesus Christ. Constantine was himself converted to the new faith shortly before he died in AD 337.

After Emperor Constantine allowed Christians to worship their religion openly, many churches were built, some of which are still in use today and have been added to by later Christians. This church was built in the early 500s, in Rome.

A triangular plaque made of silver representing a palm leaf. The 'chi-rho' sign shows its connection with Christianity. It is one of several Christian objects found at a small Roman town in England where they would have been used in religious services.

Helena, mother of Emperor Constantine. She was converted to Christianity and built many churches in Palestine on the sites of holy places. According to tradition, she discovered Christ's cross.

Fact File

The catacombs of Rome

Bodies of poor Romans were usually cremated. But early Christians in Rome preferred to bury their dead. The problem was they could not afford to build cemeteries large enough for their growing numbers. They solved the problem by digging tunnels, called 'catacombs', under Rome's streets. Thousands were buried in the passages, in slots cut into the walls which were then sealed with blocks of stone. There are over 900 kilometres of catacombs in Rome! Other cities also had catacombs. The word 'catacomb' means 'at the hollows' and it comes from a Greek word. The catacombs of Rome went out of use and were forgotten until 1578 when a landslip revealed their presence.

Inside the catacombs of Rome the underground passages are lined with niches cut into the walls. Bodies were buried in these slots and blocks of stone sealed the niches after use.

A portrait of the Emperor Constantine on a gold coin. He was responsible for the acceptance of Christianity by the Romans.

THE END OF ANCIENT ROME

The empire breaks up

This Roman fort, at Burgh Castle in Norfolk, England, was built as a defence against Saxon invaders. Many forts were built along the southern and eastern coast of Britain at this time, and experts call them Saxon Shore forts.

Why did the world of the Romans end? If only the answer was as simple as the question! Experts have argued about this for centuries and there are lots of different ideas.

Rome's problems began towards the end of the third century AD. There was fighting between army generals over which of them should become the next emperor. Fewer men could be found to join the army, and without a strong army it was harder to defend the boundaries of the empire. Food prices rose due to problems with the economy, leading to high inflation. Do these problems seem familiar to you? Many problems we have today were faced by the Romans, too!

It was difficulties such as these that weakened the empire and led to its collapse. Groups of people from warlike tribes who lived outside the empire, whom the Romans regarded as uncivilized barbarians, began to penetrate deep behind Roman defences. Their attacks became more daring and in AD 410 Rome itself was captured by thousands of Visigoths who were led by Alaric, their warrior king. The

Inside Santa Sophia. A Christian church converted to an Islamic mosque.
▼

The great church of Santa Sophia in Istanbul was built between the years AD 532 and 538. It was the most important Christian church in what was then Constantinople. It later became a mosque, dedicated to Islam. The towers (called minarets) were added in the 1500s.

Barbarian invasions

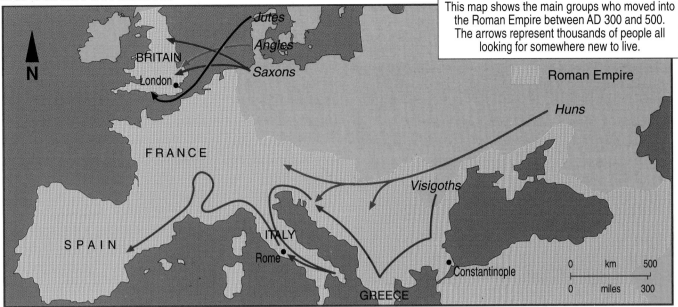

This map shows the main groups who moved into the Roman Empire between AD 300 and 500. The arrows represent thousands of people all looking for somewhere new to live.

Visigoths had been forced out of their homeland in central Europe by invaders from Asia and Russia called Huns.

The province of Britain was threatened by groups of people from northern Europe called Saxons. So the Romans reinforced their defences with new forts built along the southern coast – but when the Roman army withdrew from Britain in the early 400s, Rome's most northerly province was left open to invasion. It was probably at this time that the wealthy Faustinus family buried their valuables – no doubt hoping to return for them when it was safe to do so. But they never did return (see page 32).

Fact File

A new Rome in the east

When Diocletian became emperor in AD 284 he set about making great changes. He divided the Roman Empire into two parts – a western and an eastern empire. He knew it was becoming harder to control a single massive empire and the split was his way of solving the problem. Each part had its own emperor – but quarrels broke out between them. Then, in AD 324, Emperor Constantine reunited the empire and for a time he was the sole ruler. Constantine made even greater changes than Diocletian. He was the emperor who accepted Christianity as the state religion (see page 40), and he also moved the capital from Rome to Byzantium, a city in the east. His plan was to build a new city that would be as great as Rome. The city he built became known as Constantinople (modern day Istanbul, a city in Turkey). While Rome grew to be the centre of Christianity in the west, Constantinople became the Christian centre in the east. It stayed this way for 1,000 years, until AD 1453 when Constantinople became an Islamic city.

The city of Ravenna in northeast Italy had many fine early Christian churches. Inside they were decorated with magnificent mosaics in the Byzantine style – a style developed in Constantinople and widely copied elsewhere.

Discovering the Romans

An excavation in progress at the Roman town of Verulamium (St Albans), in England.

There are many ways to discover the Romans. Archaeologists excavate Roman sites, always on the look out for something new that can provide fresh information. A few years ago no one would have thought that a remote Roman fort in northern Britain would yield wooden writing tablets – with messages that could still be read after 1,800 years (see page 33).

But apart from finding everyday objects, how else are we discovering new facts about the Romans? One important way is to fly over farmers' fields at certain times of the year – usually when crops are growing. To the trained eye, patterns can be seen in the crops, showing the outlines of buried buildings or ancient field systems. Many Roman farms, lengths of road and even long-lost towns have been found this way, especially in Britain and France.

Archaeologists working in Italy have devised a clever way of examining Etruscan tombs without digging into them (see page 10). They push a probe deep into the ground and into the tomb. A tiny video camera sends back a picture from inside the tomb. This way the archaeologists can decide if the tomb is worth excavating – before the 'clandestini' (tomb robbers) beat them to it!

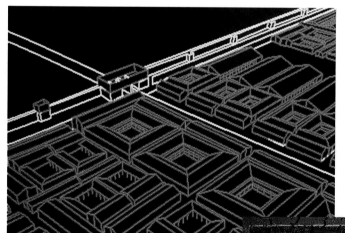

Using a computer an archaeologist can draw a three-dimensional picture of a building. This computer image shows buildings inside a Roman fort. You can also see the wall around the fort, a gateway and a road. Some of these features can be seen in the photograph of Housesteads Fort on page 22.

Roman wall paintings are very fragile and have to be carefully restored. This picture of a woman looking into a mirror has been joined together from hundreds of broken pieces, and the missing areas have been cleverly painted in.

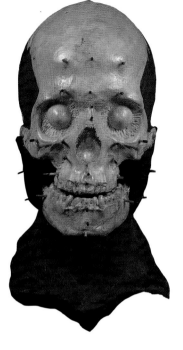

Fact File

Place names as evidence

You don't have to dig into the ground to look for signs of the Romans. Names of towns and villages can tell us if Romans used to live there. Look at this list of ten places in Britain that all have something in common. Can you see what it is?

Modern name	Meaning
1. Alcester	fort on the River Alne.
2. Chesterton	farm or village near a camp.
3. Chichester	Cissi's fort or town.
4. Colchester	fort on the River Colne.
5. Godmanchester	Godmund's fort or town.
6. Ilchester	fort on the River Yeo.
7. Kenchester	Cena's fort or town.
8. Portchester	fort by the harbour.
9. Towcester	fort on the River Tove.
10. Woodchester	fort in a wood.

In each case the name has either the word 'chester' or 'cester' in it. These words come from the Old English word 'ceaster' which means Roman camp or town. Other words, such as people's names (Cena, Cissi and Godmund, for example) were added to 'ceaster' to produce the name which is familiar to us. Place names can tell us if the Romans were in our own area. There are about 350 place names in Britain with Roman connections.

Reconstructing faces from skulls is a technique used by archaeologists and police – for very different reasons. Layers of special clay have been applied to this Roman skull by a medical artist. It is then possible to work out how the person may have looked when he was alive.

This photograph shows the outline of a Roman farmhouse buried in a field. It shows up like this because a crop will grow at a different rate if it is on top of a buried wall, where the soil is not as deep as elsewhere in the field. At ground level there may be no signs of the building at all. The straight lines that run down the picture are tracks from a modern vehicle, probably a tractor.

GLOSSARY

Amphitheatre – An open-air building used for gladiator and other shows.

Amphora – A type of storage pot for wine and oil.

Aqueduct – A narrow bridge to carry water across uneven land.

Augustus (63 BC – AD 14) – The first Roman emperor. He changed his name from Gaius Julius Caesar Octavianus to Augustus. Reigned 27 BC – AD 14.

Barbarians – Groups of people who lived outside the Roman world. The Romans regarded them as uncivilized and a danger to their rule.

Basilica – A large building at the centre of a town used by officials.

Byzantium – see **Constantinople.**

Julius Caesar (100–44 BC) – A powerful army general who was popular with the people but who was murdered by Roman senators.

Cameo – A carved semi-precious stone with two or more layers of colour.

Carroballista – A heavy-duty crossbow.

Carthage – The capital city of the Carthaginians in north Africa .

Catacombs – Underground passages in Rome used for burials and religious ceremonies.

Century – A unit of soldiers (80–100 men).

Circus Maximus – A racetrack in Rome.

Colosseum – An amphitheatre in Rome.

Constantine (AD 272–337) – The emperor who accepted Christianity. Reigned ad 312–337.

Constantinople – The city that replaced Rome as the capital. Present-day Istanbul, Turkey.

Consul – The most senior government official.

Diocletian (AD 245–313) – The emperor who divided the Roman Empire in two. Reigned AD 284–305.

Etruscans – A group of people who lived in Italy before the Romans.

Forum – A square at the centre of a Roman town used as a market-place.

Gaul – The area of present-day France and Belgium.

Gladiator – A professional fighter trained to fight to the death.

Hadrian's Wall – A stone wall in northern Britain built by Emperor Hadrian to mark a boundary of the Roman Empire.

Hannibal (247–183 BC) – Leader of the Carthaginians and enemy of Rome.

Herculaneum – City buried by lava when the volcano Vesuvius erupted in AD 79.

Insula – A block of buildings in a Roman town.

Latin – Language of the Romans.

Latium – Original homeland of the Romans.

Legion – A unit of soldiers (5,300 men).

Mosaic – A picture usually made from cubes of coloured stone.

Mount Vesuvius – An active volcano near the cities of Pompeii and Herculaneum.

Octavian – see **Augustus.**

Onager – A heavy-duty catapult.

Ostia – The port of Rome.

Pantheon – A temple building in Rome.

Patrician – A privileged, wealthy Roman.

Plebeian – An ordinary, poor Roman.

Pompeii – City buried by ash when the volcano Vesuvius erupted in AD 79.

Pompey (106–48 BC) – An army general who plotted against Julius Caesar.

Provincia (Province) – An area of the Roman Empire considered to belong to Rome.

Punic Wars – The wars between the Romans and the Carthaginians.

Romulus and Remus – The twins, who according to legend, were suckled by a wolf. Rome was named after Romulus.

Scipio (d.211 BC) – Roman general who defeated Hannibal.

Senator – One of about 600 politicians who governed Rome.

Stola – A gown worn by married women.

Strigil – A body scraper.

Stylus – A writing implement.

Tesserae – Cubes of coloured stone, glass or pottery used to make mosaic pictures.

Toga – The standard item of clothing for men.

Trajan (AD 52–117) – The emperor during whose reign the Roman Empire expanded to its greatest extent. Reigned AD 98–117.

Trajan's Column – A war memorial built in Rome to commemorate battle victories of Emperor Trajan.

Villa – A house in the countryside which was usually the centre of a large farm estate.

INDEX

Page numbers in **bold** refer to illustrations or their captions.

FURTHER READING

If you want to find out more about Ancient Rome, these books will help:

The Romans, Roy Burrell (Oxford University Press, 1991)
What Do We Know About The Romans? Mike Corbishley (Simon and Schuster, 1991)
Ancient Rome, Simon James (Dorling Kindersley, 1990)
I Wonder Why Romans Wore Togas, Fiona Macdonald (Kingfisher, 1997)
The Traveller's Guide to Ancient Rome, John Malam (Marshall Editions, 1998)
Myths and Civilization of the Ancient Romans, John Malam (Watts, 1999)
A Visitor's Guide to Ancient Rome, Lesley Sims (Usborne, 2000)